EYES

Santa Fe Writers Group

John Muir Publications
Santa Fe, New Mexico

Special thanks to Dr. Marvin Riedesel, Department of Biology, University of New Mexico, and Dr. Mary Colleen McNamara, Department of Biology, Albuquerque Technical-Vocational Institute, Albuquerque, New Mexico

Santa Fe Writers Group:
Miriam Bobkoff, research
Donald E. Fineberg
A. S. Gintzler
Miriam Sagan
Leda Silver

John Muir Publications, P.O. Box 613, Santa Fe, New Mexico 87504
© 1993 by John Muir Publications
All rights reserved. Published 1993
Printed in the United States of America
Printed on recycled paper

First edition. First printing August 1993

Library of Congress Cataloging-in-Publication Data
Bizarre & beautiful eyes / by Santa Fe Writers Group.
     p.   cm.
   Includes index.
   Summary: Describes unique features of the sense of sight in several animals, including the dragonfly, penguin, dog, crab, and four-eyed fish.
    ISBN 1-56261-121-6 : $14.95
    1. Vision—Juvenile literature. 2. Physiology, Comparative-
[1. Vision. 2. Animals—Physiology. 3. Sense and sensation.]
I. Santa Fe Writers Group. II. Title: Bizarre and beautiful eyes.
   QP475.7.B59 1993   93-13347
   591.1'823—dc20   CIP
                                     AC

Logo/Interior Design: Ken Wilson
Illustrations: Chris Brigman
Typography: Ken Wilson
Printer: Guynes Printing Company

Distributed to the book trade by
W. W. Norton & Co., Inc.
500 Fifth Avenue
New York, New York 10110

Distributed to the education market by
The Wright Group
19201 120th Avenue NE
Bothell, WA 98011

Cover photo, horsefly, Animals Animals © Stephen Dalton, Oxford Scientific Films
Back cover photo, red-tailed hawk, Animals Animals © Joe McDonald

INtroduction

A ll animals on the planet, including humans, understand the world around them by using sensory organs. The senses we know the most about are sight, smell, taste, touch, and hearing. Animals use these senses to avoid predators, to find mates, food, and shelter, and to entertain themselves. Some people believe that animals, including humans, use other, less-understood senses as well. Have you ever had a "hunch" about something that proved to be true? Maybe you were using a sense other than one of the five mentioned above.

Bizarre and Beautiful Eyes peeks inside the sense of sight in the animal world. But before we go eye to eye with the twenty animals featured in this book, let's take a close-up look at the basics of vision.

The hawk has complex, powerful eyes.

Forbes' starfish

The starfish has simple light sensors all over its body.

SIMPLE TO COMPLEX

Eyes in the animal kingdom vary from very simple light sensors to highly complex, specialized eyes. Whatever the type of eye, all sight is possible because of a substance called **visual pigment**. When light strikes the visual pigment in an eye, the pigment changes chemically. This change causes an electrical signal to be sent from the eye to the brain through nerves. The cells containing the visual pigment are **photosensitive**, which means they are sensitive to light.

The very simplest eyes are nothing more than a collection of photosensitive cells. Some animals, like the starfish, have photosensitive cells all over their bodies, but they cannot focus on distinct shapes like humans can. Other animals have basic eyes that have a **lens** as well as photosensitive cells. The lens helps the eye to gather more light and projects it onto a group of photosensitive cells behind the lens. This group of cells is called the **retina**.

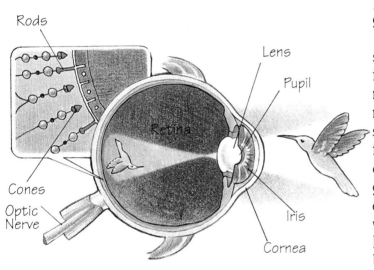

The human eye

For an animal to see a tree, a rock, or some other image, the lens in its eye must focus an image on the retina. Also, the retina must have a lot of photosensitive cells in it. In many animals, these photosensitive cells have special functions to help the eye see under different conditions. The retina of *your* eye, for example, is made up of **rods** and **cones**, groups of cells named for their shapes. Rods detect dim light and record images in black and white. Animals with excellent night vision have large numbers of rods. Cones detect color in bright light. Human eyes have 6 million cones, so we can see many beautiful colors.

The most advanced eyes, like yours, can see things that are both close and far away. To accomplish this, the eye must be able to change the shape of its lens. Specialized muscles push or pull on the lens to make it fat and round (to see things up close) or thin and flat (to see things at a distance). The lens changes shape because it needs to bend light coming in your eye so that it falls on your retina. The ability to focus on an image, to see it sharply without blurry edges, is called **visual acuity**, or **resolving power**.

In front of the lens of advanced eyes sits the **iris**, a flexible set of muscles that expands and contracts to open and close the hole that lets light into the eye. The iris is the colored part of the eye. The hole in the iris is called the **pupil**. The iris shrinks or enlarges the pupil to control the amount of light that enters the eye. In very low light, the pupil grows big to let in as much light as possible. In very bright light, it contracts to a small hole.

ELECTROMAGNETIC SPECTRUM

Different colors are made up of light waves of different lengths, or frequencies. The snake can see very low-frequency light waves, called **infrared**, which produces heat. The honey bee can see very high-frequency light waves, called **ultraviolet**. The full range of light frequencies is called the **electromagnetic spectrum**.

Infrared   Visible spectrum   Ultraviolet

The range of colors humans can see is only a tiny slice of the full spectrum. We cannot see infrared or ultraviolet rays, or those light frequencies beyond them.

Compound Eyes

Insects and crustaceans (such as crabs and lobsters) have eyes that are made up of hundreds of little lenses grouped together, each backed by its own photosensitive cells. These are called **compound eyes.** When a fly sees you with its compound eyes, it does not see only one image of you: it probably sees hundreds of the same image of you. Compound eyes cannot focus clearly on an object, but they are very effective in detecting motion, especially in dim light.

Most birds have monocular vision only.

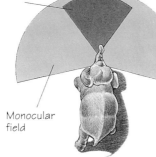

An elephant's monocular visual fields overlap to give the animal binocular vision over its trunk.

The compound eye of a dragonfly

Monocular and Binocular Vision

Many animals have eyes on the sides of their heads that scan the horizon on each side and move independently of each other. This is called **monocular vision**. In the sea horse, for example, one eye can look up while the other looks down, one right while the other looks left. This is very important to animals that need to watch out for predators—they can see more of what is going on around them than we can. The area each eye scans is called its **visual field**.

Humans and many other species have two eyes on the front of their faces that always move together in the same direction. The result is that both eyes see the same image. This is called **binocular vision**. This can be very helpful, for two reasons. First, since both eyes see the same image, together they see it much more clearly than one eye would alone. Second, since both eyes converge toward nearby objects, the eyes are better able to judge distance. This is called **depth perception**. To see how important depth perception is to you, put an eye patch over one eye and walk around the room. Do you have trouble telling how far away objects are?

This book can only give you a glimpse of all the fascinating things there are to learn about eyes and vision. But it will introduce you to many of the interesting ways animals relate to their environment and to each other. We hope this book sparks you to learn more about eyes and vision. You'll find a list of suggested reading at the end. If you want to review a term (*monocular vision*, for example), or if you come across a word you don't understand (what's a *cornea*?), turn to the glossarized index at the back. But first, let's enter the bizarre and beautiful world of eyes.

STarfish

(Class: Asteroidea)

Although they are not fish, most people call these sea stars by their common name—starfish. Marine biologists, scientists who study sea life, named these creatures "asteroids," which is Greek for "like a star." Starfish have photosensitive cells all over their bodies that react to light. Imagine being able to sense light from head to toe, just as your sense of touch covers your whole body. In the same way, starfish have light receptors from tip to tip of their many arms. They cannot, however, see distinct shapes and objects, like fish or rocks.

Near the tip of their arms, which usually number five, is a place called the eyespot, or optic cushion. If you shine a light on this eyespot, the starfish moves its arm. If you shine a light on the entire starfish, some types retreat but most creep forward. Almost every species of starfish (and there are more than two thousand!) moves in a predictable way.

The starfish does not really know it reacts to light anymore than it knows that it has just started to move. This is because it doesn't have a brain. Instead, its photosensitive cells connect to nerve cells. These nerves, in turn, send a message to the arm muscles: "Get going!" Its muscles react automatically (a reflex), and the starfish begins to creep over the rocks and sand of its watery home.

Ochre starfish

CLAM UP

A month-old starfish can devour more than four dozen young clams in less than a week! But if they cannot see them, how do starfish find their prey? During its ocean-floor patrol, the starfish uses its sense of touch to "see" food—a clam, for example. The suction power of the starfish's arms pries open the clam's shell. The starfish then positions its stomach right on top of the opened clam and starts munching. No wonder fishermen who harvest clams, oysters, and mussels want to keep starfish out of their fishing beds!

EYESPOT

TENTACLE

TUBE FEET

The arms of the starfish are covered with photosensitive cells and tipped with an eyespot. The tube feet are used for walking and for prying open the shells of molluscs.

Starfish, facing page

SCallops

(Chiamys opercularis)

What has one hundred unblinking, bright blue eyes that sit around the rim of its shell? The scallop, of course. The scallop is a shellfish, a small, soft-bodied creature that hides inside its distinctive fan-shaped shell. Its tiny eyes alternate with tentacles in two rows all around its shell. What makes the scallop's blue eyes so bright? The thin mirror-like lenses of their eyes reflect the blue of the surrounding sea, making them sparkle like shining sapphires. With eyes pointing in every direction, the scallop keeps a careful watch on its underwater world.

The main thing the scallop is on the lookout for is the starfish—humans aren't the only ones who find scallops delicious! Luckily for the scallop, it is not as helpless as it looks. Although its eyes probably do not see distinct shapes, they are sensitive to movement. If so much as the shadow of a starfish passes over the scallop, the two sides of its shell snap shut. When a starfish approaches, the scallop springs into action. The scallop is an excellent swimmer. Its method of locomotion (movement) is to shoot water out from between its valves and leap forward. With its alert eyes and ability to dart away, the scallop can escape the starfish.

Scallops are sociable creatures and gather together by the thousands in clean sand beds. They live in warm seas throughout the world.

Deep sea scallop

HEAD IN THE SAND

The scallop is a member of the mollusc family. Its cousins include the octopus, slug, oyster, and cockle. The cockle spends much of its time nestled beneath the sand. A safe place to hide, but how does the creature watch out for hunters, especially hunters that dig? The cockle has small eyes that sit on top of stalks. It can raise its eyes right out of the sand and look around, just as if its eyes were a periscope on a submarine.

The scallop shoots water out from between its valves and leaps forward to escape its main predator, the starfish.

Queen scallop, facing page

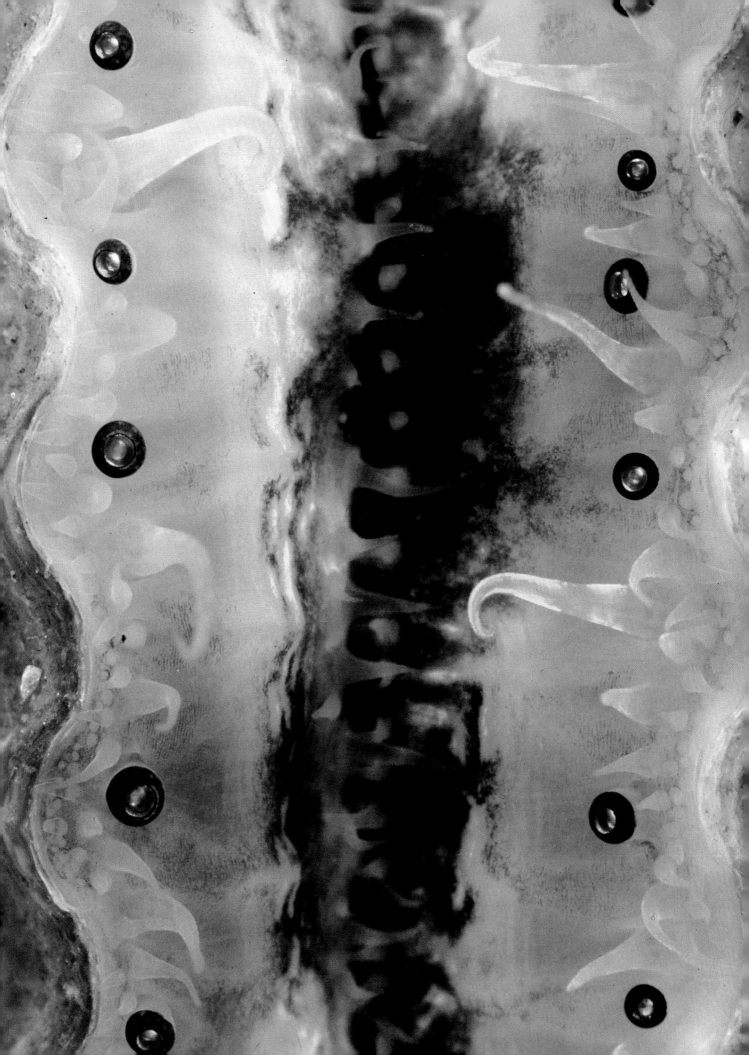

Spiders

(Order: Araneae)

A wolf spider slowly creeps toward its insect prey—then suddenly darts forward, lunges, and bites its victim. Wolf spiders are hunting spiders, dependent on their eyes for survival, unlike their web-building cousins. Web-spinners do not have keen eyesight. They sit and wait for the movement of prey caught in their webs, then follow the vibrations to attack. Hunters such as wolf, fisher, and jumping spiders, however, sight prey with their sharp eyes—all eight of them.

Most spiders have eight eyes, arranged in pairs in two rows on their heads. Unlike the compound eyes of insects, spider eyes have a single lens. One pair, the principal eyes, can move and focus on objects because they have retinas. The other three pairs, called secondary eyes, do not move, but they take in more light than the principal eyes.

The principal and secondary eye pairs serve different purposes. In jumping spiders, the secondary eyes react first, detecting movement. The spider's legs then begin to move and it turns to face the movement source. The secondary eyes then send messages to the brain about the object's distance, and the spider begins creeping forward. Next, the principal eyes scan the object in sight to determine what it is. If it's an insect, the spider will attack. In the hunter spider *Olios*, each pair of secondary eyes sees a different field of vision—forward and down, upwards, and to the rear sides. Many spiders even have eyes that see behind their heads.

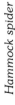

Hammock spider

ANCESTRAL ARACHNIDS

Did you know that spiders are not insects? They're officially called arachnids, along with scorpions, ticks, and mites. Arachnids are animals without backbones (invertebrates) that have four pairs of legs. The arachnid ancestors of today's spiders probably had both compound and single-lens eyes. Most likely, the spider's principal eyes evolved from basic eyes, and the three secondary eye pairs came from a splitting up of compound eyes. The earliest spiders were probably all web builders and did not depend much on their eyes for their survival. But with evolutionary changes, some spiders ventured away from the web and developed larger, more sensitive eyes and better acuity for hunting.

Most spiders have eight eyes arranged in two rows on their heads. One pair of eyes can even see behind their heads.

Jumping spider, facing page

Beetles

(Order: Coleoptera)

Elder borer beetle

There are a quarter of a million types of beetles—so many, in fact, that these insects make up 80 percent of all species on Earth. Beetles live in jungles, cities, deserts, lakes, and just about everywhere else except the open sea and the icy continent of Antarctica.

With so many types of beetles, it's no surprise there are many different kinds of beetle eyes. There are small-eyed beetles and beetles whose eyes are so big they take up most of their head. Certain beetles can see colors, and a few can even sense infrared light that humans cannot see. Some beetles, like the whirligig, have eyes divided into lobes that allow them to see above and below at the same time. Some beetles see best in bright light, others in dim light. There are even beetles with no eyes at all that live deep in the soil and in caves, where no light ever shines. They detect passing meals (smaller insects) with long hairs that can feel the air move beside them.

Like other insects, beetles have compound eyes made up of hundreds of tiny lenses that aim light toward the beetle's retina. When light hits *your* retina, it forms a clear image that is upside down. Inside the beetle's eye, the image is right side up, but it is out of focus.

LIGHT UP

Fireflies are not flies at all, but beetles that make their own light. And glowworms are not worms, either. They are beetles, too—wingless, female firefly beetles. Beetles such as fireflies are one of the few animals able to produce light. This ability is known as bioluminescence (bio means life, and luminescence is a fancy word for light). Different species of fireflies flash their lights differently. One type can even produce two different colors! The beetles' flashing "code" is their way of recognizing members of their own species. All young fireflies can light up—it's part of their mating behavior—but not all adults can.

With a quarter of a million species of beetle, it's no surprise there are many sizes, shapes, and types of beetle eyes.

12

Convergent lady beetles, facing page

Seahorses

(Genus: *Hippocampus*)

What looks like a horse but is actually a fish? The unusual sea horse. This interesting creature has excellent monocular vision. Its two eyes move independently of each other. One eye may be looking straight ahead, searching the underwater forest for a tasty snack, while the other checks behind to make sure no morsel has escaped notice. Each of the sea horse's eyes can look up, down, forward, backward, or simply straight ahead. The eyes protrude (bug out), which adds to the creature's strange appearance.

Like other fishes, the sea horse has no eyelids—which is why it sleeps with its eyes open. As it vanishes into a jungle of underwater plants, the sea horse's eyes keep a vigilant watch on the changing underwater environment. But the sea horse itself is difficult to spot. Some sea horses can even change their own color when light conditions in the water change. They can match a lighter or darker environment and blend in with grasses, sponges, and coral.

Its eyes make the sea horse a spectacular hunter of its favorite food, small crustaceans. Like the African chameleon, whose eyes move in the same independent way, the sea horse remains still and camouflaged in the seaweed before darting out to snatch a meal. Sea horses have a hearty appetite. A tiny newborn can eat up to 3,000 crustacean larvae in a morning! When the sea horse is not trying to escape becoming someone else's meal, it moves up and down in the ocean depths, as if it were riding an elevator.

Caribbean sea horse

DEEP DARK SEA

It is more difficult to see underwater than on land, as you may have noticed the last time you opened your eyes in a lake or swimming pool. Underwater light is scattered, and darker in the daytime that it would be on the surface. Like land animals that hunt at night, a fish's eye must collect enough light for its brain to process images. Fishes' retinas have large groups of rods bundled together, giving their eyes better vision in their dark underwater environment.

The sea horse's protruding eyes work independently of each other and can look up, down, sideways, backward, or simply straight ahead.

Atlantic lined sea horse, facing page

FoUr-EyeD Fish

(Anableps anableps)

This small freshwater fish resembles a minnow—except for its eyes, of course. The four-eyed fish actually has only two eyes, but each eye is divided in two by a band of skin. It spends most of its time just under the surface of the water, the top half of each eye peering above the waterline. With the top part of the eye, it watches for bird predators; with its lower eye, which is adapted for underwater vision, it watches for prey. When the four-eyed fish spots a meal, it dives down to catch it, then zips back up to the surface.

Though divided in two, the *Anableps'* eye has only a single, oval-shaped lens. But this lens does double duty, acting like bifocal (two-lensed) goggles that aid sight both in and out of water.

The *Anableps* was originally thought to be the only true four-eyed fish. But another fish, *Bathylchnops exilis*, was recently discovered in the deep waters of the Pacific, where it lives as far down as 3,000 feet. At that level, light is the blue of twilight on a winter evening. Millions of rods in the *Bathylchnops'* retina make it sensitive to the dim light. Wide vision and keen sight help this quickly darting fish catch its prey. The *Bathylchnops'* two eyes are bifocal; the lower lens of each eye gazes downwards and has its own retina. Behind these small eyes are two even smaller eye-like organs (which lack retinas). They probably serve to bend light into the pair of large eyes. Further research may reveal why this deep-sea creature needs two eyes . . . or rather, four . . . or is it six?

SURFER DUDE

The four-eyed blenny (*Dialommus fuscus*) lives on the rocky coast of the Galapagos Islands. Its eyes are divided in two by a vertical (up and down) band. It eats small crustaceans when it leaves the rocks at low tide. Then this 3-inch-long surfer rides the crest of a wave safely back into a crevice.

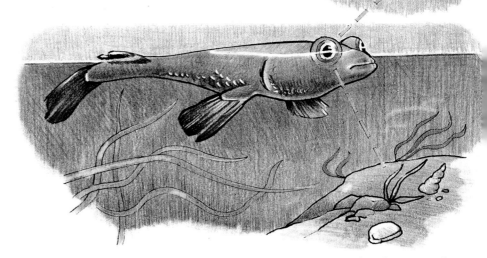

With eyes divided in two by a band of skin, the four-eyed fish uses aerial vision to watch for predators and underwater sight to search for prey.

Anableps, above and facing page

Dragonflies

(Order: Odonata)

If you've ever been around a lake or a pond on a summer day, chances are you've seen dragonflies darting about—flying in one direction, hovering, then darting off again. What are they so busy doing? Hunting—what else?—for food like flies, gnats, mosquitoes, and even butterflies. The dragonfly's large compound eyes sit on either side of its head. These eyes are keenly adapted to seeing movement, especially of small objects like flying insects.

Most critters in the insect world have compound eyes (remember the beetle?). Magnified, they look something like a honeycomb. A compound eye is made up of hundreds of tiny lenses, all pointing in a different direction. Each lens acts like an individual eye. If a dragonfly were looking at you, for instance, it would see hundreds of tiny images of you. Compound eyes are very sensitive to movement. This is because the movement is seen by each and every lens. If a friend waves at you, your single-lens eyes see one motion. The dragonfly would see a flutter of movements as the wave was projected on each and every one of its lenses.

Compound eyes can't move like our eyes. Instead, a dragonfly "scans" its environment without moving its eyes or its head. Because dragonflies attack their prey from below, they need to see best at an angle looking forward and up. This is why the lenses in the upper portion of a dragonfly's eye are larger; they have greater acuity (ability to focus) for hunting. It's interesting that helicopters—which look like mechanical dragonflies—tilt forward in fast flight, and their domes point up, just like dragonfly eyes.

Common sympetrum

cone through which light is focused

light sens cells

len

QUICK EYES

Dragonflies hunt on the fly and often eat their prey without bothering to land. Their compound eyes are therefore adapted to perceive quick movement and direction. An insect that flies across a dragonfly's visual field sets off a flicker pattern of light signals across the eye. The dragonfly's brain is sensitive to the exact timing of these signals.

A dragonfly's compound eyes are made up of hundreds of tiny lenses. Each acts like an individual eye. Together, they send a mosaic-like image to the insect's brain.

Aeschna cyanea, facing page

18

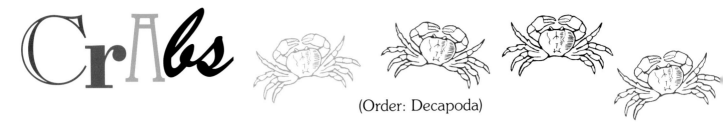

CrAbs

(Order: Decapoda)

Horned-eye ghost crab

As a rule, crabs have excellent vision. The eye of the horseshoe crab (*Limulus*) evolved many thousands of years ago, making it one of the most ancient eyes in the animal kingdom. Like insects, horseshoe crabs have compound eyes. These sit on top of its armored shell and can see as clearly at night as during the day. Imagine if you stepped out on a dark, moonless evening and could see your neighborhood in almost as much detail as if the sun were shining brightly. This is how well the horseshoe crab can see its nighttime world. It uses ultraviolet light to see when the sky is dark. Incredibly, the crab's brain sends signals to its eyes at dusk and at dawn to increase the creature's vision in dim light.

The horseshoe crab does not use its sharp eyesight to find food, as you might expect. Instead, it uses its vision to select a mate from among the crowds of crabs who gather on the sandy shores of the eastern United States.

The eyes of the ghost crab (*Ocypode ceratophthalmus*) perch on top of thin stalks on the crab's head, enabling the crab to see in all directions. Each eye is made up of thousands of photosensitive cells. These cells help orient the crab towards the sun and, scientists suspect, also towards the dimmer light of the moon.

DANGER IN SIGHT

Fiddler crabs, like ghost crabs, are very alert to their environment. This helps them to escape water birds like egrets who might be looking for a tasty bite of crab. The Indian fiddler crab can sense an egret at a distance of 25 feet (about 8 meters) and will not wait for the bird to come closer before it scurries off for cover. Deep-water and cave-dwelling crabs have less accurate eyesight. Touch and vibration are more important to them than good vision.

The horseshoe crab uses its vision not to find food but to choose a mate out of the crowd of crabs on the shore.

Sand crab, facing page

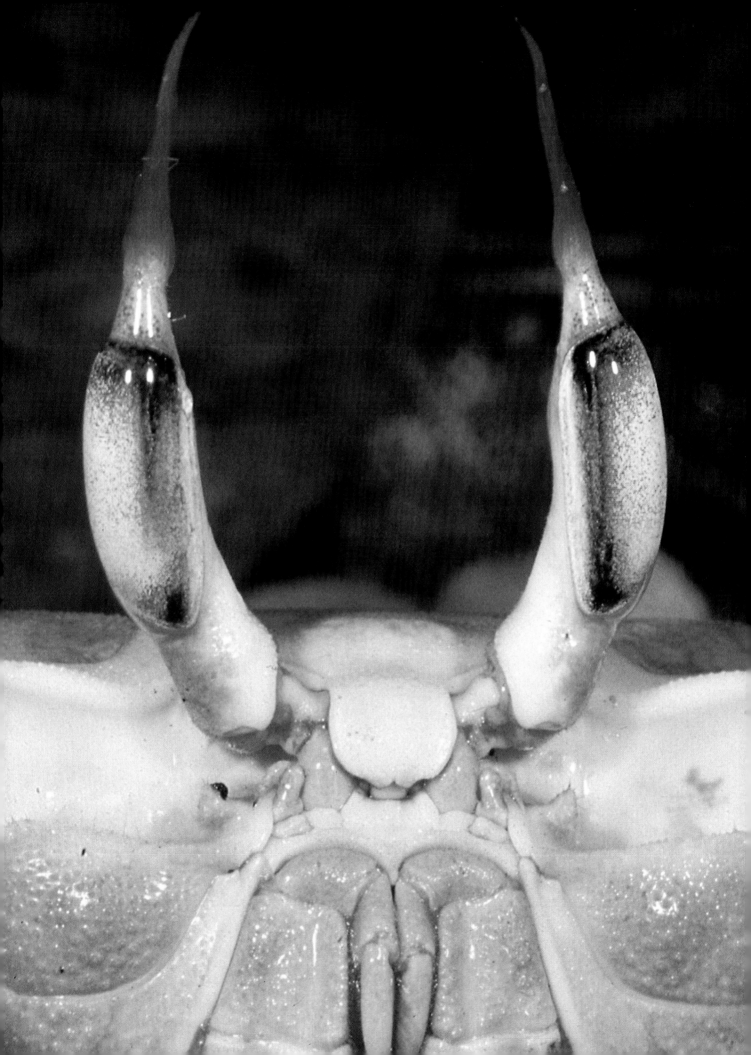

SNakes

(Order: Squamata)

Have you ever seen a snake blink? No—because they can't. Snakes have no eyelids. Their eyes are always open, even when they sleep. How are their eyes protected and cleansed? A thin transparent skin covers their eyes with a veil of lachrymal liquid, a technical term for tears.

When the snake molts (sheds its skin), it sheds its eyecovers, too. At this point, they are no longer clear, but opaque, like a fogged up window. Sometimes the snake rubs itself against trees or rocks to help slough off the old skin. Sometimes it sheds its skin in one piece, like a child wiggling out of sleeper pajamas.

Vision is the dominant sense in snakes. It is very keen in all but burrowing types of snakes. The lens of the snake's eye focuses accurately within a somewhat limited range. Snakes that hunt by day have rounded pupils. Snakes that hunt at night have vertical, elliptical (oval) pupils, similar to those of a cat. Elliptical pupils admit or shut out light more efficiently than round pupils. Snake eyes are sensitive to even the slightest movements—such as those made by the small creatures that make up their diet.

P.S. Snakes are probably color-blind.

Parrot snake

FEEL THE HEAT

How does a snake "see" to hunt in the dark? It senses heat. Pit vipers and rattlesnakes sense the infrared radiation given off by their warm-blooded prey. These "eyes" are the pit organs, two deep cavities located on the snake's head under and in front of the eyes. Heat-sensitive nerve fibers send messages to the snake's brain. In North America, other snakes with this infrared "vision" are the cottonmouth (water moccasin) and copperhead. Pythons and other distant relatives of pit vipers also have heat-sensitive pits. Instead of just one pair, though, they have many pits, sometimes more than a dozen, on scales bordering their mouths.

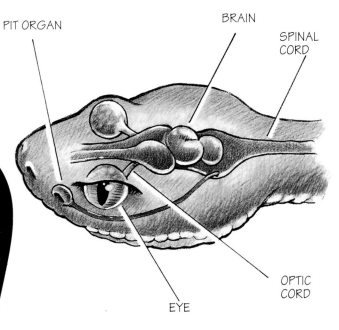

PIT ORGAN

BRAIN

SPINAL CORD

OPTIC CORD

EYE

Many species of snakes have pit organs, cavities on their heads that sense tiny changes in temperature. These heat-sensitive organs help them detect the movement of warm-blooded prey.

Eye of Indian green tree snake, facing page

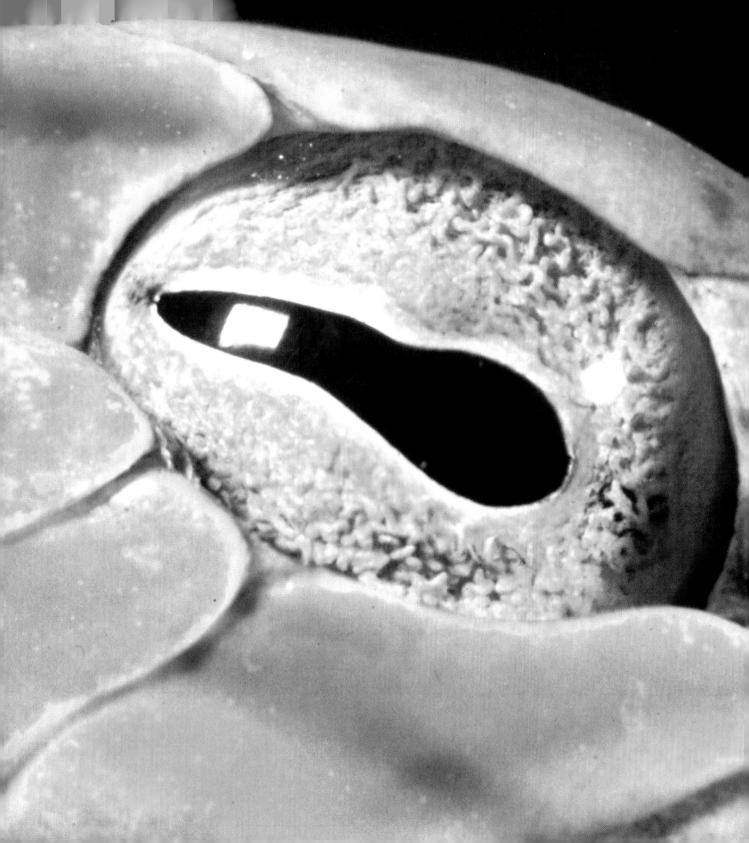

FROGS

(Order: Salientia)

Green tree frog

Frogs sitting at the edge of a pond aren't waiting for a beautiful princess to come by and kiss them. No, they're waiting for food, and food in the frog world means insects. Frogs usually keep very still, always on the lookout for visual signals from assorted flying and crawling bugs and worms. Frog eyes respond well to light and to the movement of small passing objects—especially to their favorite passing objects: insects. Frogs will eat something only if it moves; they ignore motionless objects. In fact, one group of researchers could only get their frogs to eat if they served them wriggling worms by hand! Then they found an easier way. They put bits of hamburger on a lazy Susan turntable. The frogs snapped at the moving food as it spun by!

Frogs' large, bulging eyes give them a very wide field of vision. Each eye's field of vision overlaps with the other, giving the frog binocular vision and good depth perception (the ability to judge distance). Frogs estimate the size and location of moving prey before flashing their long sticky tongues to catch it. A frog will not try to catch an insect that's too far away. Instead, it turns its body toward the insect and waits until the prey is within "zapping zone"—the length of the frog's tongue and reach.

EYE STRIPES

The colored iris of a frog's eye, like yours, expands or contracts to enlarge or shrink the size of the pupil. This adjusts the amount of light that enters the eye. But the iris is also a camouflage device. Different frog species have irises of different colors. Often, these colors blend with a frog's facial pattern to help conceal the frog.

In some frog species, eye color is a camouflaging device. Markings on the frog's body, like stripes, may continue right through the iris.

Asiatic horned frog, facing page

Chameleons

(Family: Chamaeleonidae)

These lizards are among very few animals with both monocular and binocular vision. The chameleon's exceptional eyesight helps it spot the small insects that make up its diet (locusts are a favorite). Independently of each other, its two huge eyes scan the area for possible prey. Once the chameleon spies an insect with one eye, it turns its head and, now using binocular vision, focuses both eyes on the target. The chameleon then creeps toward its next meal, stopping when it comes within its long tongue's reach. (In some chameleons, that's as long as their body and tail combined.) Then—ZAP! The chameleon's sticky tongue shoots out to snatch the insect.

The chameleon aims and shoots its tongue straight ahead with amazing speed and accuracy. Then it withdraws its tongue and bunches it up inside its mouth, like a sweater pushed up at the sleeve. The chameleon depends on a lightning quick attack for its survival—if its tongue simply lolled out of its mouth, the insect would escape. But a fast tongue is not enough. The chameleon relies on its acute (sharp) vision to judge the distance and position of its prey.

Chameleons' powerful eyes are protected by thick scaly eyelids that are shaped like cones and cover the eyes at all times. How can the lizard see with its eyes closed? There is a small hole in the middle of each eyelid, over the iris. The chameleon looks out this tiny "window" to see.

BLENDING IN

Have you ever heard someone described as a "chameleon"? It means that person changes from situation to situation—just like the lizard. Responding to cues from light and temperature, chameleons can change the color of their skin. Usually chameleons assume colors that allow them to blend into their environment and hide from predators. But when fighting or threatened, they may display bold, brilliant colors—perhaps to "psyche out" their opponents. Most species of chameleons are found in Africa and Asia.

A chameleon spies an insect and—ZAP!—snatches it with its long sticky tongue.

26

Jackson's chameleon, facing page

DOGs

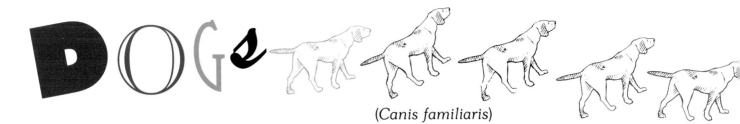

(Canis familiaris)

Most puppies are born blind, deaf, and totally helpless. A puppy's eyes are actually perfect at birth, but it takes about ten days for the eyelids to open. No one is exactly sure when puppies develop the full adult range of sight, but in most dogs it seems to be at about six weeks. That's also the usual time puppies are weaned and begin to bond with their human companions.

And just how well do adult dogs see? Not very, according to scientists who have studied dog vision. For starters, dogs are near-sighted and have astigmatism, which means distant objects appear blurry to them. Dogs are also partially color blind. They *can* see shades of blue and grey, but they confuse green, yellow, orange, and red as the same color. Dogs do, however, have excellent peripheral vision and are sensitive to motion. A dog will have no trouble spotting a rabbit bolting for cover out of the corner of its eye.

Of course, most dogs have a keen sense of smell to help make up for their mediocre vision. Even so, there are certain dogs known as "sight-hunting hounds," like greyhounds, Irish wolfhounds, and Afghans. These dogs are lean and swift, able not only to sight their prey but to pursue it with amazing speed. Sight-hunters are among the most ancient breeds of dogs. Pictures of them have even been found painted on the temples and tombs of Ancient Egypt.

Labrador retriever

GLOW IN THE DARK

Have you ever seen a dog's eyes shine when light hits them? Dogs, cats, and other animals that hunt at night have a reflecting layer behind their retinas. It acts like a piece of aluminum foil and reflects light back out of the eye, giving the animal better night vision.

Caught in the glare of headlights, a dog's eyes radiate an eerie yellow light. This is caused by the reflecting layer inside the animal's eye.

Husky eye, facing page

OCtoPus

(Octopus vulgaris)

The octopus is an extraordinary creature who has gotten a bad rap. Far from being the ferocious sea monster of sci-fi movies, the octopus is a very shy, intelligent creature. In fact, it has the largest brain of any invertebrate, which is an animal without a backbone. The octopus has eight tentacles (arm-like appendages) that help it crawl and swim and grasp food. Like its cousin the scallop, the octopus has a focusing lens in each eye that helps it both detect movement and judge distance. If several crabs are swimming nearby, the octopus will always make the right choice and grab the nearest one.

The octopus's good eyesight combined with its evolved brain allow it to learn simply by watching, rather than doing. When researchers train one octopus to do something, all the others pick up the behavior through observation. Some captive octopuses even figure out how to escape from their tanks.

In many animals, the ability to see color is linked to the ability to change color; animals that can camouflage themselves usually also can see a broad spectrum of colors. This is true of the octopus. The octopus changes color by squeezing pigment sacs located all over its body. Detecting rapid shifts in the hues around it, the octopus hides itself from predators in the nooks and crannies of underwater rocks.

GENTLE MONSTERS

Maybe you've seen horror movies in which gigantic squids fight with whales or squash submarines in their enormous tentacles. Although squids, cousins of the octopus, are much gentler in real life than in these movies, they do have an alarming appearance. This is partly due to their unusual eyes. Although they have one normal-looking eye, some squids also have a large tube-shaped eye with a yellow lens that points upward, giving it a wider field of vision.

The octopus has good depth perception, which means it can judge distance. If several crabs swim by, the octopus will always grab the nearest one.

30

Lesser octopus, facing page

Owls

(Order: Strigiformes)

When it comes to sight, owls have the best bird's-eye view. No other birds can compete with an owl's ability to see in the dark *and* see great distances. No other birds have eyes as big in relation to their face and body size. Owls' wide eyes sit on the front of their flat faces, like ours do; like us, they have binocular vision. But unlike human eyes, owl eyes cannot move in their sockets. For peripheral vision, owls swivel their flexible necks as much as 270 degrees—about three-quarters of a circle.

Owl eyes are unique in many ways. Owls see clearly in very low light. This is because their retinas are packed with many light-sensitive rod cells and their pupils are exceptionally large, letting in lots of light. In fact, owl eyes gather light three to six times more efficiently than human eyes. Owls can also see details of objects at great distances. (Some owl species are even far-sighted; they see most clearly objects that are far away but have trouble focusing on what's up close.) Combined with their swift flight, owls' acute sight makes them extraordinary night hunters. They are able to spot—and pounce on—field mice and rabbits even when they're hidden by brush or darkness. Their acute sense of hearing also helps them hunt at night.

Because an owl's eyes are so important to its survival, it has developed ways to protect them. A clear layer called a nictitating membrane covers the eyes when an owl flies through dense brush or struggles with prey. This membrane also serves to clean the eye and the inside of the eyelids. Each eye has two lids, the upper one for blinking, the lower one for closing when the owl sleeps.

Barn owl

BRIGHT LIGHTS

The great horned owl has no trouble looking directly into a clear sky on a sunny day. It never squints, as we do in the glare of bright sunlight. In fact, it can stare straight at the sun without discomfort or damage to its eyes. This is because its pupils are vertical slits, similar to a cat's pupils, and don't admit as much light as round pupils like ours.

Because owl eyes cannot move in their sockets, owls have evolved flexible necks that can turn 270 degrees—three-quarters of a circle.

Great horned owl, facing page

Penguins

(Family: Spheniscidae)

Penguins are birds who can't fly, but they can swim and dive with Olympic style. They hurtle into the freezing waters of the Antarctic Ocean to catch fish and crustaceans. They remain close to the surface and usually stay underwater for a minute or less—although Emperor penguins have been known to submerge themselves for nearly twenty minutes. Penguins have heavy bones and flippers instead of wings. Everything about them is equipped for diving.

The world a penguin sees is quite different from the world you see. This is because a penguin's eye is adapted perfectly for seeing underwater. When a penguin dives into the ocean, it sees its watery environment very sharply. The tough muscles around the iris make the penguins eye especially strong. Penguins also have good peripheral vision so they can watch out for underwater predators, such as the black and white orca (a type of whale). Visual pigments similar to those in fish eyes let the penguin see color, the seascape hues of violet, blue, and green. But that's not all. Penguins can see well into the ultraviolet range of the electromagnetic spectrum, beyond what is visible to humans.

King penguin

CLOSE UP

With its unique flat cornea, the penguin's eye is adapted for excellent aquatic vision. It is able to see distinct shapes underwater and can focus on what's right under its beak. This comes in handy because the penguin can't grasp with either its flippers or its webbed feet. It takes food directly with its beak, so it must be able to focus on objects up close. On land, the penguin might be a bit near-sighted because of this feature.

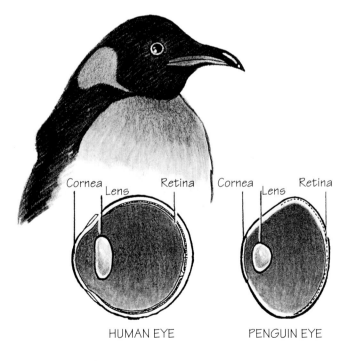

HUMAN EYE   PENGUIN EYE

The penguin is the only vertebrate (animal with a backbone) that has a flat cornea. This feature helps it see well underwater, where it hunts.

Chinstrap penguins, facing page

CATS

(Family: Felidae)

You shine a flashlight under your bed, and two yellow eyes shine back at you . . . . Is it some mysterious creature? Yes—your pet cat! Like many of their wild cat cousins, house cats are nocturnal hunters. Their shining eyes reflect light for better night vision. The reflecting layer in cat eyes is behind the retina. Light that passes through the retina without being absorbed is reflected back again, giving the retina another chance to catch the light. As it passes back out the eye, it creates the spooky shine you see in your cat's eyes.

There are other features of their eyes that strengthen cats' night vision and light-sensitivity. A cat's cornea and lens are both larger and more curved than in the human eye. This makes it possible for a greater number of receptor cells in the retina to be stimulated by light. Cats' retinas also have more layers of light-sensitive rod cells than ours do.

Cats use light 50 percent more efficiently and can see six times better in low light than humans. But their visual acuity is poor. This means that while cats can see more of their surroundings at night than humans can, what they see is out of focus. Why? Because the reflecting layer in the cat's eye blurs the image. The great number of rod cells in the cat's retina also decreases its focusing power. Because their eyes are so sensitive to light, cats' pupils have evolved as vertical slits. These pupils have special muscles that shut out unnecessary light better than round pupils do.

Serval

ANYTHING THAT MOVES

In the wild, large cats like lions, tigers, lynxes, and leopards hunt for their food. So do domestic felines—given half a chance. For this reason, cat eyes have adapted to detect extremely slight movements—such as dinner making a run for it. It's no wonder kittens pounce on anything that moves!

Cats see six times better in low light than humans, but the images they see are blurry.

Lion cub, facing page

H a W ks

(Order: Falconiformes)

Hawks build nests in the tops of trees, but they hunt from even higher elevations. With vision eight times more powerful than ours, the hawk can spot prey from great height, in great detail. Circling on its powerful wings, the hawk can clearly see the plump field mouse foraging in a field far below; all we would see is a blurry speck—if we could see it at all! Hawk vision is one of the keenest in the animal kingdom. If that field mouse tries to make a run for it, the hawk can follow it, for its eyes can detect slight movement as well as distant objects. Although they look small from the outside, hawk eyes are large in proportion to their bodies, set deep in their head.

Hawks and falcons can be trained to hunt. (A falcon is a hawk with long wings.) When fully trained, these raptors (birds of prey) will leave their perch, hunt their prey, then return to their trainer. This sport is called hawking or falconry. More than 2,500 years ago, the ancient Assyrians caught and trained hawks. And during the Middle Ages, kings and noblemen enjoyed the sport of hawking. After the invention of the shotgun about 400 years ago, men took to hunting with guns instead of birds, and the sport of hawking declined.

INVISIBLE ENEMY

Even a hawk's sharp vision cannot detect the bird's deadliest enemy: poison. Some farmers use poisons called pesticides to protect their crops from pests such as insects and rodents. Birds that eat the poisoned pests become ill, and sometimes sterile as well (unable to produce young). Even hawks that usually live far from human beings are in danger because they stop to feed when they migrate. There, on a peaceful farm, the hawk may meet its invisible foe.

Far up in the sky, a circling hawk spots a plump mouse in the grassy field below. With vision eight times more powerful than human sight, it sees its tiny prey in detail.

Red-tailed hawk, above and facing page

Elephants

(Elephas maximus and *Loxodonta africanus)*

Believe it or not, it's the elephant's trunk that is responsible for the evolution of its eyes. When you look at an elephant from the side, you see just one of its eyes. An elephant has monocular vision, each eye scanning the horizon on its own side. But if you look at an elephant face on, it will look back at you with both eyes pointing forward. This kind of vision is binocular, like yours.

Elephant eyes are adapted for monocular *and* binocular vision. The question is, "why both?" The answer is, "the trunk." If elephants only had monocular vision, they could not focus in front of their faces, where their trunks do their business. Elephants use their trunks (also called a proboscis, from the Greek word for nose) for more than just breathing. They use them to grasp leaves from treetops, to feed themselves, to spray cool water over their backs, and to move objects out of their way. While monocular vision lets an elephant keep an eye on its side surroundings, binocular vision allows the animal to keep track of its trunk.

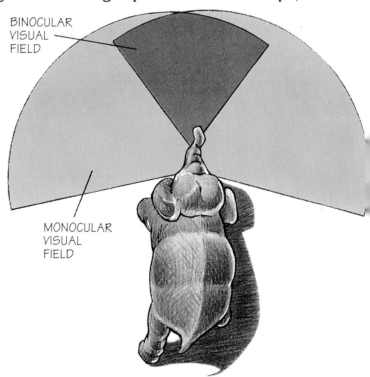

The monocular visual field is the area each of the elephant's eyes sees on its own. The binocular visual field is the area the eyes see together when they look forward.

African elephant, facing page

SIZING THINGS UP

When it comes to eye size, elephants take the prize. No other land mammal has eyes as big as an elephant's. Only whales, which are sea mammals, have eyes that are bigger. Yet, in proportion to the size of the elephant's body, its eyes aren't really all that big. Horses and zebras are ten times smaller than elephants, but their eyes are almost as large.

Zebras

(Genus: *Equus*)

Zebra eyes are adapted for one main purpose: spotting danger. Set far back and wide-apart on their long faces, zebra eyes have a very wide angle of vision. With a sweep of their head, they can take in a panorama of their native African savanna. Even while grazing, zebras keep watch above the grass tops with their high-set eyes. When a zebra spots a predator, such as a lion, its defense strategy is simply to run—fast!

Located on the sides of the head, each zebra eye has a monocular visual field of 146 degrees(about a third of a circle). When the zebra points its eyes forward, these fields of vision overlap for binocular vision. Working together, the eyes share a binocular field of 65 degrees (less than a quarter of a circle). This is much narrower than the binocular field of carnivores (meat-eaters), who need good depth perception to hunt. Zebras are herbivores (plant-eaters) and feed on grasses.

Like cats, dogs, and other animals, zebra eyes have a reflecting layer that increases the amount of light absorbed by the rods in the retina. Zebras can therefore see extremely well at night. They don't, however, focus as quickly as most animals do. Instead, zebras see long and short distances out of different parts of their eyes. To bring images into sharp focus, zebras use the upper part of their eyes only.

Burchell's zebra

DON'T BE SHY

Zebras and horses are cousins, both members of the genus *Equus*. Have you ever wondered why wagon horses wear blinders, leather flaps that block the animal's side vision? Horses, like zebras, have wide fields of vision, but their eyes focus slowly. The sudden movement of a bird swooping or a car speeding by therefore can startle a horse and cause it to bolt or rear. This is called "shying," and it can be dangerous. If a horse shies on a busy street, for example, it may dart in front of a moving car. Blinders help horses focus calmly on what's ahead.

Even while grazing, zebras keep a lookout over the grass tops for predators, such as leopards.

Grevy's zebra, facing page

Humans

(*Homo sapiens*)

Your eyes are amazing things. They weigh less than one ounce (7 grams) each and measure only an inch across (2.5 centimeters). Yet they provide four-fifths of all the information received by your brain! Humans depend on sight more than any other sense. In fact, sometimes our vision overwhelms our other senses. Try this: Listen to the sounds around you. Now close your eyes and listen again. Did you hear more the second time?

Light enters your eye through the cornea and passes through the pupil and lens. The retina receives the image—upside down. Once there, the rods and cones in the retina turn it into a visual signal (called an impulse) to be sent to the brain via the optic nerve. The part of the brain that handles vision is called the optic center. Once the optic center receives the visual impulse, it perceives it as a meaningful image (and turns it right side up). The optic center is located at the base of the brain, which is why an injury to the back of the head can cause blindness or impaired vision.

Because your eyes are so very important, they have ways of protecting themselves. Tears wash your eyes of irritating dust and even help kill germs. And if an object suddenly flies at your eyes, you will automatically blink to shield them. But sometimes these natural protections are not enough. You should never look directly at the sun because the bright light can damage your retinas. And you should always wear goggles when building something or working with machinery.

WINDOWS OF THE SOUL

Eyes have been called "the windows of the soul" because they communicate our feelings—sometimes even when we don't say a word. Do your eyes sparkle when you're happy? Do they narrow when you're mad? What does a wink mean? Why do couples in love gaze longingly into each other's eyes? Look in the mirror. What do your eyes "say"?

About five kids in a hundred have a "photographic memory," the ability to remember in detail an image they saw a long time ago. By the time they grow up, most of these kids lose this ability.

Human eye, facing page

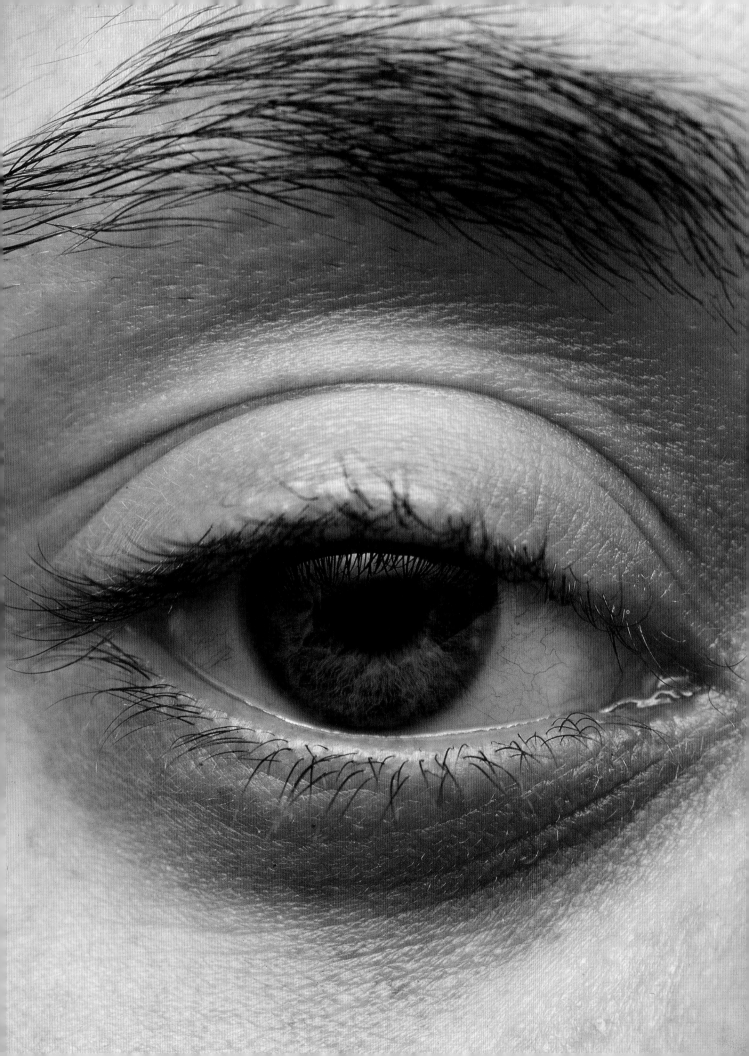

GLOSSARIZED INDEX

This glossarized index will help you find specific information about the sense of sight. It will also help you understand the meaning of some of the words used in this book.

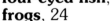

Other books about animals and the five senses:

Amazing Animal Senses, Ron Van Der Meer, Little, Brown & Company, 1990, 0-316-89624-1

Animal Senses, Jim Flegg, Newington Press, 1991, 1-878137-21-2

Extraordinary Eyes: How Animals See the World, Sandra Sinclair, R.R. Bowker, 1991, 0-8037-0806-8

Fingers & Feelers, Henry Pluckrose, Watts, Franklin, Incorporated, 1990, 0-531-14050-4

Tongues & Tasters, Henry Pluckrose, Watts, Franklin, Incorporated, 1990, 0-531-14049-0

Touch, Taste & Smell, Steve Parker, Watts, Franklin, Incorporated, 1989, 0-531-10655-1

Why Do Cats' Eyes Glow in the Dark?: (And Other Questions Kids Ask about Animals), Joanne Settel & Nancy Baggett, Atheneum-MacMillan, 1988, 0-689-31267-9

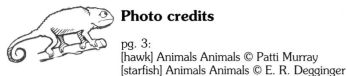

Photo credits